POSITIVE

VIBES

Stay Positive!

PRESTON MITCHUM

PM.

Positive Vibes

© Copyright 2019 Preston Mitchum

ISBN: 978-1-941345-61-0
ASIN: B07XD68BTX

ERIN GO BRAGH Publishing

Canyon Lake, Texas
www.ErinGoBraghPublishing.com

INTRODUCTION

No matter what is going on around Preston Mitchum, Jr., he looks for a positive perspective on the situation. He celebrates the good times and looks for ways to learn through the tough ones. His message is clear:

POSITIVE THOUGHTS, POSITIVE VIBES.

Having developed a nice following, along with encouraging and enlightening so many friends and associates with his uplifting words, it occurred to him that there was a necessity for sharing these messages with those that were not connected to him.

What a way to connect the world, through a readership and daily inspirational that is designed to enlighten us with positivity.

Whether you read these messages back-to-back, or every once in a while, the goal is to help boost your perception of life, take time to appreciate it and find the positives that are all around us.

God has given us such an amazing gift - this life. Let's show our appreciation for it by cherishing each and every moment.

2 Corinthians 9:15

Thanks be to God
for His indescribable gift!

TABLE OF CONTENTS

LET'S TALK

Are we truly connected or disconnected? In a society where technology has taken over, the word "conversation" takes on a different form. Texting, emails etc. is how we communicate now. What happened to the old fashioned face-to-face conversation and taking a few minutes to call someone and chat it out?

Understanding each other through text can be misinterpreted and lack emotion. Is this the type of connection the world needs? As humans, we carry emotions and that's how we express ourselves. Through speaking and body language we can best interpret what someone is saying.

Whether positive or negative the best interpretation is what we all need.

POSITIVITY

IS

PRECIOUS

A POSITIVE START

How do you start your day; a cup of coffee, exercise, meditation, reading?

We all have something or some way to start the day. It's important to take a little time in the morning to balance yourself for the day. If, your goal is to give your best, you must be your best.

Find that something that can help you start your day off right. How you start your day can play a major part in how it wraps up.

POSITIVE THOUGHTS, POSITIVE VIBES!

CHOOSE THE LIFE YOU LIVE

We all have control of the type of life we want to live. Most of us would love to live a happy life filled with positivity. Of course there will be some bumps in the road, but our choices decide that.

Also, things that you have no control of will try to consume you. Allow how you would like to live to lead the way.

Take a few minutes every morning to balance yourself with positive thoughts that will keep you on the right path. Remember you have the power to live the best life you want.

POSITIVE THOUGHTS, POSITIVE VIBES!

POSITIVE ENERGY

How do we attract positive energy? It's not always easy but it's all about perception.

Learn to see the positive in any situation. Let go of your perceived control or the need to be in control.

We all have the ability to allow positive energy within. I mean seriously, who really wants to live in negativity? Put yourself in positive situations, around positive people, think positively and let your light shine.

POSITIVE THOUGHTS, POSITIVE VIBES!

FREE YOURSELF

Be free, feel free.

It's no fun waking up every morning thinking about fifty million problems to solve. Or carrying around burdens and guilt about something you said or did.

You are the only one who can free yourself from it all. Allow at least a few moments a day to feel free.

Some problems you will have to let go of and understand that we don't always say or do the right things. You give the world YOU; the best you have to offer. That has to be good enough!

POSITIVE THOUGHTS, POSITIVE VIBES!

LIVE FOR TODAY!

People spend so much time worried about the future. It's something that we really don't have any control over. Instead of worrying about the future, why not create it?

Play your part in positively creating the change you want to see now. That will lead into the future. Get up and start doing what you can in order to see the results you want.

Tomorrow is not promised but we all have hope to see the sunrise in the morning. Yes, tomorrow is a new day and you can start working on that right now.

POSITIVE THOUGHTS, POSITIVE VIBES.

DAILY AFFIRMATIONS

What a beautiful day!

It doesn't matter if it's sunny or raining, hot or cold, the Lord gave you the chance to enjoy this day, so go ahead and do that.

FEELING SAFE

What does it mean to feel safe? Is it the ability to be yourself completely without judgement? This can be very difficult because the world is full of judgement.

Planet fitness says it best:
"Welcome to the judgement free zone."

Put yourself around people and in environments that will accept you for you.

When you feel good about yourself, the world is getting your best. Family, friends etc. will see and feel your spirit and accept the true you. As we continue to grow and accept ourselves, we tend to judge others less.

POSITIVE THOUGHTS, POSITIVE VIBES!

SWITCH ON THE LIGHT

My father used to say, "You can't see unless you turn on the light."

We all have a switch and an opportunity to turn on our light. Allow your light to see you through the dark times.

Troubles don't last forever
and your light is always there.

POSITIVE THOUGHTS, POSITIVE VIBES!

DAILY AFFIRMATIONS

*God gave us another
beautiful day my friends.
Share a smile
and some positive vibes.*
Stay blessed!

PEACE & PROSPERITY

YOUR PEACE

Take yourself to a place of peace; a place where the wind blows and animals roam. It's a place that's far away from the hustle and bustle of the everyday chaos. It is where the living is easy and the thoughts have time to collect.

Today is your day to find your peace.

What makes your mind rest and your heart sing? You owe it to yourself to have that experience, if not forever, at least for a short moment.

POSITIVE THOUGHTS, POSITIVE VIBES.

FEEL THE PEACE

Feeling peaceful is not allowing negative thoughts or energy to take over. Surround yourself with inspiring people and positive things. Take some time to declutter your mind and allow your soul to feel at peace.

POSITIVE THOUGHTS, POSITIVE VIBES!

John 16:33

I have told you these things, so that in me you may have peace. In this world you will have trouble. But take heart! I have overcome the world.

13

HOW DO WE ACHIEVE PEACE?

What does the feeling of peace feel like?

Have the courage to change the things you can and understand the things you cannot. It is the ability to let go, and let God lead you. There are many things that will distract you from achieving some type of peace.

Find a way to have less control and allow life to just be.

Take time to breathe and be still.

This will declutter your world and get you closer to achieving peace.

POSITIVE THOUGHTS, POSITIVE VIBES!

14

Ecclesiastics 3:12-13

*I know that there is nothing better
for people than to be happy and to do
good while they live. That each of them
may eat and drink, and find satisfaction
in all their toil—
this is the gift of God.*

YOUR HOME

They say home is where the heart is. My oldest son, Carter, will ask "Daddy, what are we doing today?" I answer, "Not sure, what would you like to do?" He replies, "Stay home."

There is a comfort in being in the space you call home. It is a place where you feel love, safe and at peace.

Many of us search all of our lives looking for a place we can call home. Sometimes, the space is right in front of you. The simplicity of it is what we should look for.

Home is where the heart is so let your heart be at home.

POSITIVE THOUGHTS, POSITIVE VIBES!

A GIFT FOR YOURSELF

We all love getting gifts. What was the best gift you ever got? Was it something big or small? An article of clothing, nice card, new TV, flowers; the list goes on. The best gift may be spending some time with yourself.

Take some time to get to know you again. Taking time out to reconnect from within is a gift of inner peace. The feeling you get will help to cleanse and energize your soul.

There is no gift someone can give you that will feel better than connecting with yourself.

POSITIVE THOUGHTS, POSITIVE VIBES!

THE GREAT OUTDOORS!

My youngest son, Harrison, loves being outside, whether he's catching bugs or looking for slugs late at night, being outdoors makes him happy.

God's little creatures can offer a sense of gratification. Whether it's riding scooters, or swinging on a swing, take a few minutes to enjoy the peacefulness of the outdoors. It's simplistic, no drama, no over thinking.

Nature allows you to just be and enjoy what life has to offer. You might be surprised how good it makes your spirit feel.

POSITIVE THOUGHTS, POSITIVE VIBES!

PEACE IN THE MIDST OF STRUGGLE

The world we live in looks like a mess sometimes. Crime, poverty, drugs; every time you turn on the television it's bad news.

Our lives can also be a mess, having us spinning around like a spinning top. Sometimes it's best for us to be still and stop thinking about our problems.

A moment of peace might allow you to see the problem differently and provide a new approach. That approach might provide some peace in the midst of the struggle and hopefully let you rise above.

POSITIVE THOUGHTS, POSITIVE VIBES!

Job 3:26

I have no peace, no quietness;
I have no rest, but only turmoil.

MAKE TIME FOR PEACE –
IT IS YOURS FOR THE TAKING.

LOVE YOURSELF

TO

LOVE OTHERS

LOVE YOURSELF

How do you respect and love yourself?

People come into our lives all of the time. When we respect ourselves, we show them how we would like to be treated. When we love ourselves, our true selves will shine bright for the world to see.

It is up to us to understand that we're not here to be accepted by everyone. God made you in the form He wanted. Love and respect who that person is and look within.

POSITIVE THOUGHTS, POSITIVE VIBES.

POWER OF LOVE

We meet people for a reason. They can become a blessing or a lesson on our journey. Taking the time to understand one another is a form of LOVE. Our differences become less obvious and the unknown more common.

There is an old saying, "Love thy neighbor," and we are all neighbors looking for the same thing in life. There is an opportunity to show love and be loved.

Share a little love today. Offer a smile, a kind word or a helping hand. Fill your soul with positive energy and you will experience the power of LOVE.

POSITIVE THOUGHTS, POSITIVE VIBES!

DAILY AFFIRMATIONS

Tolle said it best my friends.

*"Life is the dancer,
and you are the dance."*

LOVING YOU

Dance like no one is watching. Love like there is no tomorrow.

Love comes from the heart which affects the mind, body and soul. We all love something or someone in our life time. How we interpret, accept and/or run from it is up to us. Love what you do and feel the passion.

Believe in yourself and give your all or you may never know the possibilities. Give of yourself and enjoy the happiness of loving.

POSITIVE THOUGHTS, POSITIVE VIBES!

WHERE THE HEART IS

There is an old saying, "Home is where the heart is." This can have so many meanings and it really depends on how you want to interpret it.

Is it the place you feel safe, loved and/or at peace? Is it the physical house you live in or that special place you go to reconnect? Or, is it that special someone you are willing to move around the world with because you feel at home with them?

In this crazy world, just knowing where home is, is very important. Allow your soul to feed your heart and that will provide peace in whatever you feel is home.

POSITIVE THOUGHTS, POSITIVE VIBES!

OFFER YOUR HEART

Trust your heart and it will never steer you wrong. The mind may play tricks on you but the heart never will. Yes, the road you travel will be bumpy, allowing a few scars along the way. These are the not-so-pleasant times of your past.

If you trust your heart, follow it, and more than likely, the outcome will be what was meant to be. Let that light of yours shine and allow your heart to tell your story. The world is ready for what your heart has to offer.

POSITIVE THOUGHTS, POSITIVE VIBES.

DAILY AFFIRMATIONS

Share some love and
Be a LIGHT today!

Let your light shine!

FILL YOUR SPIRIT WITH LOVE

Be the smile you want to see,
be the love you want to feel.

We all have the ability to bring a little sunshine in the world. Your attitude and approach on life can make or break your day.

The energy we give is the energy we will receive. Your light tells the world that positivity is within. This will drive out the negative energy and fill your spirit with the love it needs.

POSITIVE THOUGHTS, POSITIVE VIBES!

GIVE YOUR SOUL!

One of the greatest gifts someone can give is their soul. It means they completely trust you, and feel comfortable with who you are and where you are.

The ability to be vulnerable from within, and allowing your feelings to be shared can be terrifying. It means sharing your deepest thoughts, wants, desires. The effects of life experiences have shaped you. You are a different person today than you were yesterday.

Hopefully you will be blessed with that opportunity to be freed, in order to be free.

POSITIVE THOUGHTS, POSITIVE VIBES

WE'RE ALL CONNECTED!

Should we just be focused on our own needs and not the needs of others? Within this universe of ours we find different ways to connect or disconnect. It doesn't matter where you come from, who you are or where you are going; we all need to connect.

When you let your light shine, it allows others to connect. When you open yourself up, you give others permission to explore the true you. That's when the connection begins, and where it leads can be a positive mystery.

POSITIVE THOUGHTS, POSITIVE VIBES

DAILY AFFIRMATIONS

Wake Up!

*Open your eyes
and receive the blessing
that God has for you today.*

BECOMING

~ YOU ~

BE KIND

Today is your day to be kind. A single act of kindness can have a positive rippling effect.

Share of yourself and the next person may share with someone else. People talk about karma. What we do now can come back to affect us later.

It's not about being self-absorbed but rather, giving of yourself which will allow a peaceful spirit to take over. Being kind frees your spirit and unlocks the chains and negativity.

POSITIVE THOUGHTS, POSITIVE VIBES.

BE YOU!

Most of us spend our time trying to live a perfect life. Or, might I say trying to fit in with the latest styles, home, car, the list goes on. When seeking the perfect life doesn't work, some turn to drugs, alcohol and other toxic devices. Just find a way to live your life.

God has a life just for you!

The journey is yours and not everyone or everything is meant to be in it. Be you! Love the life you have and continue to add positive things to it. It will be an awesome feeling when you feel good about you!

POSITIVE THOUGHTS, POSITIVE VIBES!

Job 39:13

*The wings of the ostrich flap joyfully,
though they cannot compare with the
wings and feathers of the stork.*

FINDING YOUR PATH

How important is it to you to find your path? Our purpose in life is something most of us want to understand. Should we spend most of our time searching for this? Will we stumble on it by accident?

Making peace with yourself, accepting yourself and believing from within is key. Live your life and your path will be what it will be. Your view of the present will offer a positive outlook on the future.

POSITIVE THOUGHTS, POSITIVE VIBES.

QUOTE OF THE DAY

"Life isn't about finding yourself.
Life is about creating yourself."

George Bernard Shaw

YOUR PRIORITIES

What are priorities? Things that are urgent can cloud our priorities. Nothing shapes us more than focusing on the need and not the want.

A person on their death bed sees the world differently. Understanding that every moment is precious, the foggy glasses become very clear. The priorities become simple and the journey less rocky.

Take a step back and allow the power of the now to help you focus on what is important.

POSITIVE THOUGHTS, POSITIVE VIBES.

DAILY AFFIRMATIONS

*Don't be afraid to be different
my friends, Just Be!*

*God gave us another day
to get it right.*

Enjoy!

40

DREAM

Dreamers, keep on dreaming! Who said that your dreams are not possible?

Yes, we don't know the future but if we stay in the now we can understand ourselves. Grab what you know and start with that. The road will get hard and you might not know where to turn. Just pick up the pieces and reclaim what is yours.

Most successful people have stumbled a few times. So, stand up tall and don't allow anything or anyone to knock you down.

You've got this!

POSITIVE THOUGHTS, POSITIVE VIBES!

FREE YOUR SPIRIT

No one knows what you have been through or what you have seen. Whatever you have conquered, let it shine through your soul.

Allow your spirit to run free and the sparkle in your eyes to shine bright. You may never know the impact you will have on another.

When your soul smiles, you wear a glow that will attract positivity. You control what you allow in and out.

POSITIVE THOUGHTS, POSITIVE VIBES!

YOUR TIME IS NOW!

There is a reason that you are still here. What does being still here really mean?

Your thoughts, beliefs, dreams and vision of the life you want are still here. They are still in the present waiting for you to start living.

Are you stuck? Stuck in the "what if" zone?

Get up and start living. Put that plan in place and move forward. Leave those troubles behind and put your positive hat on.

Your time is now!

POSITIVE THOUGHTS, POSITIVE VIBES.

2 Corinthians 10:12

*We do not dare to classify or
compare ourselves with some who
commend themselves. When they
measure themselves by themselves
and compare themselves with
themselves, they are not wise.*

THE STORY OF YOUR LIFE

YOUR MOMENT IS NOW

We are all blessed with our own voice, a gift, and a story to tell. Share it. More importantly, listen. Listen without condition, without ego.

Is there something you have always wanted to do? Don't allow negative energy to hold you back from doing it.

Seize the moment!

You have the power to positively impact the world. Look deep down into your soul and let your light shine. Reflect.

Someone is waiting for YOU!

POSITIVE THOUGHTS, POSITIVE VIBES!

START LIVING

God only gives us one life. What do you plan to do with yours? Don't spend most of the day complaining or thinking about the negativity.

Get your butt up and start living. Live for you first and the rest shall follow. Life doesn't have to be that difficult.

Do what's right, treat people fairly and laugh as much as you can. There is nothing more beautiful to hear than the laughter from a child. Remember that as you plan out your life.

Laugh like a child
and live like there is no tomorrow.

POSITIVE THOUGHTS, POSITIVE VIBES!

THE PAINTER OF YOUR STORY

Living within our universe and painting the picture we show the world will create a canvas filled with different colors blending into one story. Your story!

We all have a picture to paint and hopefully the world will accept it. If not, remember God has a plan just for you. You are the painter and your story needs to be shared. Someone, somewhere will see, hear and feel who and what you are.

The connection with those will honor your pathway that God has planned for you.

POSITIVE THOUGHTS, POSITIVE VIBES

WHAT'S SHAPING YOUR STORY?

We all have a story. Most of it comes from past experiences or simply the past. Our parents and grandparents share their stories which help mold and shape us. But, the here and now plays an important role in our current story.

We have the ability to reshape what the next chapter will be. We might not know the ending but the pathway we choose can lead us to a positive ending.

POSITIVE THOUGHTS, POSITIVE VIBES.

WHO ARE YOU?

Do we really know who we are? The person that people see, is that really the true you or a facade? It's not always easy to give the world the true you.

Our true selves are forever evolving because we are always in growth mode. Through growth, we understand ourselves better; feeling more and more comfortable in our own skin.

Just love yourself!

Love what you know about yourself and share that with the world. The ones who truly appreciate it will see the beauty in you!

POSITIVE THOUGHTS, POSITIVE VIBES!

OUR PURPOSE IN LIFE

It is a good question and sometimes, we are not sure what the answer is. YOU hold the answer to what your purpose in life is. Your vision becomes clear when you tap in and look within. Most people work all their lives and dislike what they do.

Passion is the driving force to your dreams and the ability to be happy. Seek what you love and what you are passionate about.

Try to find what makes you feel alive and turn your passion into reality. Sing a song and allow the music from within to guide you.

POSITIVE THOUGHTS, POSITIVE VIBES!

CHANGING YOUR PERSPECTIVE

Some might say you woke up this morning on the wrong side of the bed. Are your plans just not working out the way you want them to?

When things are going wrong, what do you do? Throw in the towel or turn a negative into a positive?

Look at the small things and start there. You might be able to take care of a few little things to get your day going. Challenges can be chances for you to view things differently.

Taking a different perspective could turn your day around. There is a reason for everything; take a step back and breathe.

POSITIVE THOUGHTS, POSITIVE VIBES!

WHAT IS YOUR PASSION?

Your passion will take you to places you have never been before. When you allow it to take over, nothing and no one can hold you back.

To some, it may be work or a chore but to you, it is you. The things you are passionate about order your steps in the direction of happiness. What you feel inside is like nothing else. To be honest, it's sometimes hard to even put it into words.

Passion is a beautiful thing that lives in all of us, it's time to let your passion shine!

POSITIVE THOUGHTS, POSITIVE VIBES.

TRUST YOURSELF

Trust the you from within. Tap in and understand who you are and what you will become. Things happen for a reason, things happen at a time and place when least expected.

We are all traveling a road where there is unknown. Trust your gut, and understand the road is long, but good. Yes there will be a few bumps here and there but being true to yourself will help lead you in the right direction.

The good in you will be good enough and the ride will be worth it in the end.

POSITIVE THOUGHTS, POSITIVE VIBES

Ezekiel 1:28

*Like the appearance of a rainbow in the
clouds on a rainy day, so was the
radiance around him. This was the
appearance of the likeness
of the glory of the Lord.*

YOUR NAME

We all have a name but what does yours mean to you? Your name can mean so many things to you and the ones you're connected to. Does it define who you are? Will people remember your name in the way you want?

You have the ability to shape what your name means to you and the world. We are all given a name to be proud of and to share with others. Our names connect us in ways we can't sometimes explain.

Allow the known and unknown of who you are to be a positive impact on others, through a name given by God.

POSITIVE THOUGHTS, POSITIVE VIBES.

WHAT WILL YOUR LEGACY LOOK LIKE?

How you live or choose to live will be how people view you. It's not about how much money you make or anything with material value. It lies within the character of the person you are.

You hear it often... he or she would give the shirt off their back, or, he or she always had a kind word to say.

Your positive impact will have a lasting effect on every person you meet. Let that be your legacy - one of giving, and less of receiving.

POSITIVE THOUGHTS, POSITIVE VIBES

WHAT IS YOUR TALENT?

Everyone has talent. God gives us all some type of gift. Sometimes we allow stumbling blocks to divert us off our path.

It is not always easy to analyze yourself to see and feel what your gift might be. Take a moment to think about your skills, abilities and passions.

The talent that has been bestowed upon you is waiting to be unleashed. No stress, just breathe and feel.

POSITIVE THOUGHTS, POSITIVE VIBES!

HOW MUCH DO YOU WANT IT?

We all have something that we really want to have or achieve. Whether it is personal, business or pleasure, if you really want it, you can get it.

Take a moment to write down why it's so important to you and how it makes you feel. It could be obtainable sooner or later and it can be difficult to wait.

Sometimes good things come to those who wait. Patience is a virtue. We have heard these things time and time again. Think of them as you move forward in achieving what you want and continue to move forward.

POSITIVE THOUGHTS, POSITIVE VIBES!

LET YOUR LIGHT SHINE

Today and always, may positive things fill your life. Weed out the negative and replace it with the positive.

When you let your light shine you have the opportunity to bless someone else. The energy we release will invite positivity into your life and also add something to someone else's.

As you face those challenges today,
may your light shine brightly.

POSITIVE THOUGHTS, POSITIVE VIBES!

YOU ARE IMPORTANT!

Always remember the importance of you!

Every one of us plays an important role in creating history. Our lives will not only be shaped by our experiences, but the choices we make. The life you live continues to impact the ones around even if you don't recognize it.

Someone is watching, listening and taking in your light. Allow it to shine and never underestimate your possibilities of making a positive impact.

Walk, talk and live with a purpose for the importance of you is valuable to the world.

POSITIVE THOUGHTS, POSITIVE VIBES!

I HEAR YA!

You had your life all planned out and it's not looking anything like you imagined. Married, kids, successful job, big house, fancy car, etc.... The issue is, you were moving too fast.

Remember that living in the now is always the best because we cannot predict the future. When we move too fast we forget to see all of the awesome things around us now.

You have the power to control the present which might help with the future. Live, love and enjoy what you have now and allow that positive energy to lead you into the future.

POSITIVE THOUGHTS, POSITIVE VIBES.

SPEAK YOUR TRUTH!

Don't let anyone or anything change what you feel is true to you. God gave you a voice, your voice to share with the world. Some will interrupt it as good, some not so good or, maybe just different.

If what you offer is your truth then that is good enough. The doubt brings faith and the faith brings hope. Love the life you have and keep living it. Through your truth, you will grow.

POSITIVE THOUGHTS, POSITIVE VIBES

DAILY AFFIRMATIONS

Share some love and
Be a Light today!

Let your light shine!

YOUR JOURNEY

IS MOVEMENT

YOUR JOURNEY

We all have our own journey. The question is, are you living your best life?

It's important that we focus on the simple things in life allowing us to travel a road with fewer bumps and potholes.

We tend to get caught up in the concept of what will make us happy; a nice car, a big house and trying to keep up with the Jones's.

Start from within and focus on the little things. It will put you on the pathway of living your best life.

POSITIVE THOUGHTS, POSITIVE VIBES!

THE MOVEMENT OF LIFE

Enjoy life's simple pleasures. That includes a nice cup of coffee, a morning sunrise, and a cool summer breeze. We are blessed when we can recognize those simple pleasures.

The world gets us going. It's like a rat race and we're always on the go. We start to focus on the big things or so called things of the future. Today is your day to live. Make a step forward, maybe take a step back. Or, just stop moving and be still. Maybe make a 360 degree turn and take in all of the simple pleasures around you.

Positive things are in front of you and you need to take a moment and breathe in it.

POSITIVE THOUGHTS, POSITIVE VIBES.

Judges 18:6

*The priest answered them,
"Go in peace. Your journey
has the Lord's approval.*

SLOW DOWN

Sometimes the world gets too big and we have to figure out ways to break it down so we can handle it. Sometimes it's difficult just to breathe. Find a way to keep it simple.

A quote from my favorite movie *Shawshank Redemption*, "The world went and got itself in a big hurry." Find a way to slow down, see the world a little smaller, and allow the enormity of it to simplify.

POSITIVE THOUGHTS, POSITIVE VIBES!

Reference: *Line spoken by* Brooks Hatlen *in the movie* "Shawshank Redemption", *1994*

WHAT'S FUELING YOU?

Your power lies on the inside. It's time for you to light that fire and allow your emotions to take you there. The "there" is fueling inside of you and waiting.

Use your emotions to change the way you feel, think, and act. Laugh a little. Sing a little. Maybe even pray a little. Use what God has given you to create the positive change you are seeking.

Nothing will happen until you let go and allow the power from within to take control.

POSITIVE THOUGHTS, POSITIVE VIBES!

FILL YOUR TANK

Are you running low on fumes or on empty? Do the daily tasks of the week have you feeling spent?

What will you do to rejuvenate your mind, body and soul? At the end of the day, you can only do what you can do.

Don't continue to run low on fumes and burn out. Stop and listen to your body and get those juices flowing again.

The world needs the best YOU have to offer!

POSITIVE THOUGHTS, POSITIVE VIBES!

THE ROAD TRAVELED

It's not about the destination, but the road traveled. It's not about where you are going but how you get there. That includes all of the pit stops and fill-ups along the way. These things help shape and prepare you for what is waiting.

Things always have a way of working themselves out. The pot holes, road closures and detours are a part of the journey. Continue to move forward and stay focused. You will be surprised where the road leads you.

POSITIVE THOUGHTS, POSITIVE VIBES.

THE DIRECTION OF FORGIVENESS

Dr. Martin Luther King Jr said it best, "Darkness cannot drive out darkness; only light can do that. Hate cannot drive out hate; only love can do that." Our ability to forgive is something we consistently need to work on. Forgiveness is not easy; you have to allow yourself to be vulnerable in some situations. Without forgiveness, there is no peace!

In life, we will have to forgive in order to move forward. Not only do you free yourself when you let go of the past, but you live in the now! When you take a step back to see the big picture, you understand the importance of letting go and letting God lead!

POSITIVE THOUGHTS, POSITIVE VIBES

RIDING ON A MOVING TRAIN

Not sure where you're going or what your next stop is? Did you ask God to order your steps? Yes, the train is always moving but do you know what your next stop is? Is life what you expected? Do you need more'?

Sometimes less is more and your search could be sitting right in front of you. Stop searching and moving around so much. Be still and breathe and allow the train to fuel up.

Running on fumes can cloud your pathway and put you on a road of uncertainty.

POSITIVE THOUGHTS, POSITIVE VIBES

Go, Go, Go!

The world is always on the go.

My father, being a landscaper,
often said, "Grass never sleeps."

New York City is often referred to as the city that never sleeps. The craziness of this world can have us spinning in circles.

It's not always easy to find time to even think. You must take some time out every day to be still. This will give you time to focus on your needs and not your wants.

Your priorities will align and your spirit will feel at ease.

POSITIVE THOUGHTS, POSITIVE VIBES!

DAILY AFFIRMATIONS

This world wants you to stay busy all the time. There is no time to just sit and be still. Take a few minutes to tap in today!

MAKING A
CHANGE

THE CHANCE TO MAKE A DIFFERENCE

Today is the day when you can create change.

Sometimes we're put into situations that allow us to make a difference. Big or small, the opportunity has presented itself and it's up to you to take the leap. A leap of faith into something that challenges your being and challenges your current thoughts into new ones can bring about change.

Change will happen with you or without. Don't hold back on the opportunity of positivity.

POSITIVE THOUGHTS, POSITIVE VIBES.

REFLECTIONS

Take a look in the mirror; what do you see? Our personal experiences shape how we view ourselves. Do you like what you see? Are you happy with the person you are?

Today is the day you accept yourself, love who you are, and try to embrace the changes you need to make in your life.

Bit by bit, piece by piece, you will continue to shape the person in the mirror. Looking into the mirror gives you a chance to reflect within. Love who you are because we all have something positive to share.

POSITIVE THOUGHTS, POSITIVE VIBES!

KNOW YOUR WORTH

Knowing your worth allows you to tap into your everyday power and can change your life for the better. How do you take back control and appreciate your self-worth?

Put yourself around people who see you for the person you are. The willingness to look from within is a great start. Self-worth is defined as, "The sense of one's own value or worth as a person." Because God made you, this already shows your value and worth.

Don't let the negativity of the world steal that from you. Hold your head up, let go, breathe, and spend some time in the positive zone! Know your worth!

POSITIVE THOUGHTS, POSITIVE VIBES!

CAN YOU WEATHER THE STORM?

Mama told me the road wouldn't be easy. When the storm comes your way, ask yourself, "Are you ready to stand? Are you secure in yourself to know that this too shall pass?"

You will get through this just like you got through the last one. God never gives us more than we can handle. So, stand tall, and trust that He will bring you through.

This means: HAVE FAITH!

Faith is the substance of things hoped for, and the evidence of things unseen.

POSITIVE THOUGHTS, POSITIVE VIBES!

DAILY AFFIRMATIONS

Enjoy this beautiful weather.
Eat lunch outside, go for a walk
or take a dip in the pool.

MAKE A CHANGE

Be the creator of the change you seek.

Michael Jackson said it best, "If you want to make the world a better place, take a look at yourself and make a change"

We all have the ability to create change whether big or small. Let's not look to our right or left but in front of the mirror and allow that person to create change.

POSITIVE THOUGHTS, POSITIVE VIBES!

Reference: *Line sung by* Michael Jackson *in the song "Man in the Mirror" written by Siedah Garrett and Glen Ballard, from the album* Bad, *1987*

Forget the list of things
you're supposed
to get done today...

and take some time to just BE!

GROWTH & ACCEPTANCE

GROWTH & ACCEPTANCE

Start living the life you have and not the one you had. It's in the past for a reason. Second chances are all about acceptance.

Understanding where you came from will lead you to where you are going. Moving forward is about growth. Love yourself enough to know your life is always evolving and it's best to be in the here and now.

The opportunity is yours for the taking.

POSITIVE THOUGHTS, POSITIVE VIBES.

NEW GROWTH

Are you ready to plant your garden?

First thing is to clear out all the weeds. Just like in our lives, we must weed out the ugly in order to plant something new.

Cultivate the soil, cleanse your soul and put the past behind you.

Plant those seeds and water daily. Put yourself around motivational people and read your daily devotional to feed your soul.

Take the necessary steps
and watch your growth.

POSITIVE THOUGHTS, POSITIVE VIBES.

TIME FOR NEW GROWTH

Some days you feel like all is lost. You're buried in worries, troubles, bills and more. Well, it's time to sprinkle on some new soil and allow your flower to grow.

Find a new way to look at things or grow some new roots. Turn in some of the old for something new. Make a few new friends, change jobs, move into a new neighborhood.

A change of scenery can make all the difference in how you view yourself. Planting yourself in new soil can allow your flower to grow and change your current situation.

POSITIVE THOUGHTS, POSITIVE VIBES.

Ecclesiastes 3:1

*There is a time for everything
and a season for every activity
under the heavens.*

DON'T WAIT
TO BE HAPPY

Too many people waste their lives dreaming about when they'll finally be happy.

They spend so much time waiting for that special day, that they miss each special day that they were given. Don't miss it!

LIVE IN THE MOMENT!

POSITIVE THOUGHTS, POSITIVE VIBES!

WHAT WILL YOUR ATTITUDE BE TODAY?

You have the power to choose what your attitude is. You can alter your life by changing your attitude. Your outlook and perception can not only impact you but also the people you connect with.

Is your attitude worth catching? If not, how can you tap in and make sure what you give is what you want to receive.

Maintaining a positive attitude is not always easy, but it can be done.

POSITIVE THOUGHTS, POSITIVE VIBES!

KEEP YOUR WORD!

Why is it important to keep your word? The old saying, "Your word is your bond," is important. The promises you make, or break, define who you are.

Sometimes it's best to say, "No," than to promise something you can't fulfill. Not everyone can accept, "No," but they can respect your honesty. Honesty is the best policy and the insurance it brings is priceless.

POSITIVE THOUGHTS, POSITIVE VIBES

CONTINUE GROWING

Why have you stopped growing? Most of us get stuck in what we know and not what we don't know.

Benjamin Franklin said it best, "The doors of wisdom are never shut." There's always room for growth and always something to learn. We tend to get comfortable in our lives and the daily grind, so we forget there is always something to learn.

Growth comes from wanting to know the unknown. Yes, the unknown can be scary, but if you look from within, you can overcome the fear. Your continued growth will take you places you can only dream of.

POSITIVE THOUGHTS, POSITIVE VIBES!

QUOTE OF THE DAY

"Move out of your comfort zone.
You can only grow if you are willing
to feel awkward and uncomfortable
when you try something new."

Brian Tracy

UTILIZE YOUR SENSES

SOUND OF WATER

TLC said it best, "Don't go chasing waterfalls." What's already downstream is past you. Sometimes in life, we need to slow down and allow things to unfold.

Following the wrong things or wrong people can lead you down a path of uncertainty. Your heart will never fail you and living your best life is what you need to strive for. Most people just exist, and don't take the opportunity to live.

Take a moment to breathe and listen to the sounds around you. The rain can be soothing, just like a trickling stream or the ocean. The waves can provide a simple sounding board that will keep you on the right path.

Reference: *Line sung by* TLC *in the song* "Waterfalls" *Album* "CrazySexyCool"*1994*

Deuteronomy 33: 13-16

*May the LORD bless his land with the
precious dew from heaven above and
with the deep waters that lie below;
with the best the sun brings forth and
the finest the moon can yield;
with the choicest gifts of the
ancient mountains and the
fruitfulness of the everlasting hills;
with the best gifts of the earth
and its fullness and the favor of him
who dwelt in the burning bush.*

97

LISTEN TO YOUR GUT

I woke up this morning and something said, "Listen to your gut!" What does it mean to listen to your gut?

Something deep down inside tells you that you're making the right move, and that you've found the right person. You feel like you've found the right way to go. Trust your gut and make that move.

Whether it turns out the way you expected or not, trust yourself. In our lives, we must find something or someone to trust. Look deep inside and go with it!

POSITIVE THOUGHTS, POSITIVE VIBES.

DAILY AFFIRMATIONS

*When was the last time
you just listened?*

*Close your eyes for thirty
seconds and just listen. Cars.
Construction. Birds. Wind.
Every sound is a part of life.*

SMELL THE ROSES

There's a saying, "Take some time to smell the roses." It means, take a moment and enjoy the beauty that is all around you.

This is a great way to start creating positivity in your life. Take a moment to enjoy the flowers, birds, the sunset, and a full moon. Don't run around all day and ignore what is simply beautiful around you.

Beauty represents good, and the good was created by God. Open your eyes to His creations and enjoy your ability to take it in.

POSITIVE THOUGHTS, POSITIVE VIBES.

DAILY AFFIRMATIONS

Pause to see the flowers!

If there are no flowers blooming, take a few moments to look at pictures of floral blooms. The internet is full of beauty too.

TURN OVER A NEW LEAF TODAY

Allow the wind to blow you in a new direction. God has created a pathway just for you! Open your eyes and recognize the good around and allow it to carry you through!

Proverbs 11:28

Those who trust in their riches
will fall, but the righteous
will thrive like a green leaf.

WHY AREN'T YOU LAUGHING?

They say laughing is the best medicine. Sometimes I laugh so hard that tears come out of my eyes. Laughing makes your soul feel good and sends positive energy to your mind.

I love people who tell jokes and laugh at their own humor. The ability to allow yourself to laugh is one of the greatest gifts.

Seek those opportunities to let yourself go and take in the positive energy laughing can offer.

POSITIVE THOUGHTS, POSITIVE VIBES!

DAILY AFFIRMATIONS

*You can choose to see the rain,
or the rainbow. You can choose
how you will view this day.*

Live in the NOW!

No Need

To Fear

FACE YOUR FEAR

How do you stare fear in the face? You have to look deep within and use your past experience to provide strength.

It's not easy to do or attempt something you fear. Taking the leap will not be easy but the outcome could be worth it.

You will never know what you can do unless you try. Through this process you will find out more about yourself. Build confidence in the old and new you.

POSITIVE THOUGHTS, POSITIVE VIBES.

NEVER FEAR

What are you afraid of? What is holding you back? Fear? Scared of failing? Most of us are scared, but when you look within, you have the power to overcome.

Make your determination to succeed stronger than your fears. If you don't try, you will never know your potential.

You control your ability to achieve and succeed. Remove the stumbling blocks, negative energy and give the world your best.

POSITIVE THOUGHTS, POSITIVE VIBES!

LIMITATIONS

I know, you keep getting knocked down. Every time you catch your breath, here comes something else. You ask yourself, when will it end?

Some might say life is never ending. There will always be someone to take care of or something to handle. Sounds like it's all about balance -- understanding what you can and cannot do.

Your limits are not limitations but an important warning to slow down. Your mind and body will speak to you. It is up to you to listen.

POSITIVE THOUGHTS, POSITIVE VIBES.

WHAT IS YOUR TRUTH?

Your truth is NOW, not in the past nor future. Who are you? Who do you want to be? You must live and speak your truth.

Those who want to hear you, will listen. Others will try to silence you. Live, share and express who you are without limits. It will attract those you need in your life.

Let the thoughts from your mind flow through your heart and be true to your soul. Today is the day you live the life you have always wanted.

POSITIVE THOUGHTS, POSITIVE VIBES!

DON'T HOLD BACK

Stepping into the unknown is never easy. The next chapter can be scary as hell. You have been in this situation before. Take the plunge and see what's on the other side.

They say, "You won't know until you try." Don't let fear, people, or just the unknown keep you from your blessing.

God has something special for all of us. As I've heard others say, "Step out on faith and let God lead the way."

POSITIVE THOUGHTS, POSITIVE VIBES

FEELING LOST?

Sometimes getting lost can help you find your way. Not knowing which way to turn can put you on the right path. They say, everything happens for a reason, and there is a time and place for everything.

Take a step back and let God lead. Allow Him to order your steps and He will guide you in the right direction.

Our way is not always the right way. Our plans might not be His plan for us. So you are not lost, my friend. He's just waiting for you to find Him.

POSITIVE THOUGHTS, POSITIVE VIBES!

STOP SPINNING

Do you feel like you're spinning out of control? Feel like you're stuck in a tornado with life's debris flying around you? Like you're being pulled apart in every direction at once? Do you duck when the obstacles fly towards you instead of facing them head on?

When the world seems to be barreling down on you and you feel like you are spinning out of control, take a moment to stop and breathe. Allow your spirit to rest a little today.

POSITIVE THOUGHTS, POSITIVE VIBES

LET GO OF THE PAST

Let go of the past, and stare at the future. We all carry emotional baggage. You know, that stuff we carry around from the past that affects our present. It keeps us in the past while also pushing us into the future. Then what happens is, we forget about the NOW!

Trying to get out of the mess is not always easy, but it is necessary. When you forgive, you start to let go and unlock your spirit. A free spirit will allow you to move into the present and put some of that past behind you.

POSITIVE THOUGHTS, POSITIVE VIBES.

ARE YOU THE OPTIMIST OR THE PESSIMIST?

The optimist sees the good, the opportunity and green light in everything. The pessimist might be operating with a red light mentally, and always find problems. Our lives are comprised with a little bit of both.

Not everything will be as beautiful as a bouquet of roses. There will be times when the thorns take over. Your outlook and perception is your choice. Try to see the good and beauty in most of the things you approach.

Only you have the ability to stop you. Anything is possible with the right point of view.

POSITIVE THOUGHTS, POSITIVE VIBES

EVERYTHING HAPPENS FOR A REASON

Where you were, and are now, shapes the person you will be. Can you change the past? Maybe?

Growth allows us to look at things from a new perspective. A new point of view can provide a different outlook on things from your past. Sometimes you need to confront your past fears to move into the present.

You have the power to capture the moment that will help you move into the future.

POSITIVE THOUGHTS, POSITIVE VIBES

A PROBLEM FREE LIFE

You don't always have the capacity to handle it all and you don't need to. Yes, you can take on everyone else's problems and add them to yours. Superman or Superwoman, you wear the name quite well. It could be time to start living a more problem-free life.

Recharge yourself so your mind, body and soul are ready to accept what God has in store for you. It's ok to say, "No. Sorry, I'm busy," or, "I just can't deal with that right now." If you can push a few things aside, the positive energy will have room to enter.

POSITIVE THOUGHTS, POSITIVE VIBES.

WORRY WARTS!

We have to remember that we are living in an imperfect world. There will always be something to worry about. Did you accomplish everything today? Is your family ok? How can you solve that problem in your life? It's impossible for us to take care of everything and make sure everything is perfect.

Your objective is to give your best. Understand that some problems can't be solved. Some things are not yours to worry about. Don't allow your spirit to be consumed with the negativity of the world.

Worrying too much will not move you forward. It will take you off of your path of positivity.

POSITIVE THOUGHTS, POSITIVE VIBES!

Matthew 6:25-34

Therefore I tell you, do not worry about your life, what you will eat or drink; or about your body, what you will wear. Is not life more than food, and the body more than clothes?

Look at the birds of the air; they do not sow or reap or store away in barns, and yet your heavenly Father feeds them. Are you not much more valuable than they?

Can any one of you by worrying add a single hour to your life?

REST & REJUVENATION

REST THE SPIRIT

Take care of your spirit to fuel your physical self. Your spiritual self is the most important component of your being. You must do things and surround yourself with people who energize your spirit. If your spirit feels good most times your body will follow.

Nutrition and exercise are very important as well. Balance yourself by getting your spirit in the right place. You need both your spiritual and physical self to be balanced so the world is getting the best of You!

POSITIVE THOUGHTS, POSITIVE VIBES!

DANCE OF REJOICE

Kirk Franklin said it best, "Melodies from Heaven rain down on me." In the midst of the storm, ask God to pour himself all over you.

Stand still and feel the freshness of the rain as it washes away your sorrows, fears and negative thoughts. You must let go and let God take control and get you through those tough times.

Listen to the song He has given you and dance that dance of rejoice. He will fill you up like you never have felt before.

POSITIVE THOUGHTS, POSITIVE VIBES.

Reference: *Line sung by* Kirk Franklin *in the song* "Melodies from Heaven" *Album* "Songs from the Storm, Volume 1*"2006*

REJOICE ALWAYS

1 Thessalonians 5:16-18

_Rejoice always, pray continually,
give thanks in all circumstances;
for this is God's will for you
in Christ Jesus._

A DAY OF REST

Make today your day of rest. Some days you can feel so tired, you can barely stand. The ability to get through your day and get into bed is the best feeling.

Your body and spirit need time to rest. Without rest, you find yourself spinning in circles without truly accomplishing the tasks at hand. Put a few things aside and take some time to breathe today.

Let your mind relax and fuel your spirit.

POSITIVE THOUGHTS, POSITIVE VIBES!

Show Gratitude!

*Take the time today to tell
or show someone
you appreciate them.*

Tomorrow is not promised!

GIVING
THANKS

LETTING GO

GIVING THANKS

Take some time to thank your true friends. Through the good and bad times, your true friends are there. Through growth, you can distinguish between those who are true friends and not. A best friend has lived the stories with you and will walk with you through fire. They touch your heart because they look deep into your soul. Know your true friends and it will help you figure out the ones who are not.

POSITIVE THOUGHTS, POSITIVE VIBES!

Hebrews 13:2

Do not forget to show hospitality to strangers, for by so doing some people have shown hospitality to angels without knowing it.

COUNT YOUR BLESSINGS

You woke up this morning, so thank God for the many blessings in your life.

Yes, we all have tough days but today is your day to let go of the negativity.

But remember this, it is your journey, and your blessings belong to you. Own it!

Put yesterday behind you
and move forward with today!

POSITIVE THOUGHTS, POSITIVE VIBES!

THROUGH GIVING, WE RECEIVE!

What does that mean?

Nothing feels better than allowing your spirit to give. I believe some of the happiest people are the ones who give.

Offer a kind word, help a family in need, lend an ear when someone needs to be heard. You receive by allowing positive thoughts into your soul and by letting go of the negative ones.

Your spirit is open to receive the joy that is waiting for you. Giving comes in many forms; don't stress, just be!

POSITIVE THOUGHTS, POSITIVE VIBES!

128

Be Thankful

What are you thankful for?
Take some time today and reflect
on the things that are
most important!

IS LIFE FAIR?

What would you consider fair?
Why do we need fairness?

In life you will be treated in ways that you feel are unfair. This unfairness is actually our own perception of what we consider to be fair. How we respond is key!

Can you let it go? You have control of how something or someone makes you feel. Approach the situation with good energy and let go of the negativity surrounding the circumstance. This is the perfect opportunity to let your optimistic outlook shine through.

POSITIVE THOUGHTS, POSITIVE VIBES!

Proverbs 2:9-10

Then you will understand what is right and just and fair—every good path. For wisdom will enter your heart, and the knowledge will be pleasant to your soul.

SECOND CHANCES

So if you're reading this, God gave you a second chance on life. Don't allow things of the past to bring you down!

It's your chance to put those things behind and focus on the now. Think about the things you want to fine tune about yourself and just do it.

You now have a second chance to get it right!

Go get yours!

POSITIVE THOUGHTS, POSITIVE VIBES!

PROBLEM SOLVER!

Most of us spend so much time trying to solve problems; our own problems as well as our friends' and family's problems. That's not what we are here for -- solving as many problems as possible. When you see or feel all of those problems coming your way, stop and breathe.

Understand that you are only one person and God only gives us 24 hours in a day. Sometimes it's ok to say, "No!" Make sure that you do your part in balancing your life first. This will allow you to pick the problems you are best able to tackle and the ones you don't need to.

POSITIVE THOUGHTS, POSITIVE VIBES!

TAKING ON
LIFE'S CHALLENGES

You will face moments that test your strength and willpower. These challenges can make you a stronger person and allow you to learn some valuable lessons.

Our growth comes through challenges and our ability to move forward. That's what makes us who we are. Look for the silver lining and allow a little light in to help get you through.

It's not always an easy ride, but you do have the ability to get through.

POSITIVE THOUGHTS, POSITIVE VIBES!

WORKING TOGETHER

WE ARE ONE

Fall is upon us! The trees are different sizes, and bare different colors. As we enjoy the beauty of it all, it puts things in perspective.

Our community is a melting pot of all different shades. We all blend together to form one. No matter where you came from or where you are going, we are all part of one universe.

POSITIVE THOUGHTS, POSITIVE VIBES!

Proverbs 27:19

*As water reflects the face,
so one's life reflects the heart.*

THE IMPORTANCE OF CONNECTION

Our ability to connect is so important in our day-to-day living. That connection allows us to conduct business and establish friendships.

Through growth, we understand ourselves better which allows us to continue to build positive connections; dissolving the ones that tear us down.

The best connections let you be you, which will attract the best people to travel on your journey with you.

POSITIVE THOUGHTS, POSITIVE VIBES!

DON'T GO IT ALONE

You don't have to do it all alone. Yes, there are some things that can be better done alone, but you can usually accomplish more as a team.

The ability to understand and work with others is so important. Collectively we can have a huge impact on creating change in the world.

One person can light the spark and it's up to the rest of us to keep the flame going. No matter if it's personal, professional, or community-related, reach out and encourage others to join you.

Two minds are more powerful than one.

POSITIVE THOUGHTS, POSITIVE VIBES!

WHAT MAKES
A GOOD LEADER?

Great leaders make sure to boost the morale of the ones around them.

If people believe in themselves, they appreciate what's in front of them. Leaders have to overcome obstacles, and the way they handle adversity shows the qualities of the type of leader they are.

We all have leadership abilities in us, we just have to find our pathway or calling. The task can be small or huge but don't allow YOU to stop yourself from accomplishing the impossible.

POSITIVE THOUGHTS, POSITIVE VIBES!

LOVE AND UNITY!

In this crazy world we live in, sometimes we forget that love conquers hate and unity eliminates division. We must be open to building bridges, instead of perpetuating hate, anger and ignorance.

Through love comes understanding and the ability to see past ourselves. We cannot let our egos cloud a pathway of being open-minded.

You control what you feel for others. Can you see their beauty or just their faults? Can you see beyond what might hurt and see what can heal?

Start with positivity and see what you get!

POSITIVE THOUGHTS, POSITIVE VIBES!

BEING PREPARED TO COMPROMISE

There will be times when we need to compromise for the common good. Should we compromise ourselves or just a situation or circumstance?

The ability to see the big picture can help guide your steps. Some might say, "Never sell yourself to the devil." Understand this is give and take; no one will get exactly what they want but maybe they'll get the chance to move forward.

Put the past behind and live in the now.

POSITIVE THOUGHTS, POSITIVE VIBES!

WHO WILL BE THERE?

The words of the Ben E. King song, "Stand By Me" leads me to wonder; can you be that rock for others, can you be that shoulder to lean on?

We all need someone or someone who can be there in our time of need. Whether it's your father, mother, sister, brother or friend. It's truly a blessing when you have that rock. The person who stands strong and keeps you upright.

God will send you an angel. Open your eyes and recognize the beauty in it. The energy will put you back on the positive track in life.

POSITIVE THOUGHTS, POSITIVE VIBES.

Reference: Ben E King *song "Stand By Me" from the single released in 1961*

DAILY AFFIRMATIONS

*Soak up the sun
and sing your favorite song!*

Know that YOU are Blessed!

A CHILD'S LOVE

And a child shall lead them. One of the greatest gifts God gives us is children. Pure and innocent, they come into the world just needing love and guidance.

This is also one of the greatest responsibilities as well. As parents, you give your all and in return they give you unconditional love. Love for our children comes in all different forms and wanting the best for them is universal.

Allow their purity and innocence to help lead your steps. You will be surprised how much you will learn.

POSITIVE THOUGHTS, POSITIVE VIBES!

PEOPLE PLEASER

Are you always trying to please others? Do you find yourself getting lost in taking care of everyone else?

Yes, it's good for us to help others but also wise to take care of ourselves. Your spirit must have time to rejuvenate itself in order to handle what life throws at you.

Without a strong self, your ability to help will be limited. Your ability to make the right choices and decisions could be clouded. Let go and let God lead your thoughts and guide your steps. He will help you decipher what you can do and what you should do.

POSITIVE THOUGHTS, POSITIVE VIBES!

BE TRUE TO YOU

Are you living a life that is true to you? God wants us to have heaven on earth. Is this possible? Of course, it is! Keep it simple and be YOU!

Your ability to understand who you are and what you have to offer should be your priority. Don't try to be someone others want you to be. Be a good person, give your best and love life.

Don't focus on the afterlife, but the present life. Don't judge, but love what you feel in the now. Control what you can and let go of what you cannot.

POSITIVE THOUGHTS, POSITIVE VIBES!

Colossians 3:16

*Let the message of Christ dwell among
you richly as you teach and admonish
one another with all wisdom through
psalms, hymns, and songs from
the Spirit, singing to God with
gratitude in your hearts.*

FOR THE TAKING

Sometimes people come into our lives at the right moment. It could be just that simple. It can be simple enough to enjoy the moment, to take what is given you and to allow it to be.

Over thinking and over analyzing can lead you off the pathway meant for you. This is your time to grow, love and share, what is being offered.

Everyone will play a role. The closing act is yours for the taking.

POSITIVE THOUGHTS, POSITIVE VIBES.

148

No Judgement Day

Let's make this a no judgement day! Don't judge yourself, don't judge others.

Romans 14:13

Therefore let us stop passing judgment on one another. Instead, make up your mind not to put any stumbling block or obstacle in the way of a brother or sister.

YOU ARE BLESSED

Did you forget that you are blessed? Just stand still and think of all the things you have. Food, shelter, a job, a sound mind, and the list goes on.

Stop focusing on what you don't have and be thankful for what you do have.

Your perspective and perception could be the key to seeing the blessings in your life. As the song goes, "Every time I turn around, blessings on blessings." God wants you to have heaven on earth. He's giving you blessings.

So, pause and accept what He has for you.

POSITIVE THOUGHTS, POSITIVE VIBES.

Reference: *Song by* Anthony Brown *and Group Therapy*

VICTORY!

My mother sang a song in church, "Victory is Mine." What would you consider your victory? Are you on the right path and have the right mind set to enjoy your victory?

Remember it's all yours! How you feel, think, love and live, belongs to you. Your victory is waiting for you to enjoy and it will unfold itself when your soul is ready.

Don't go looking for it because it might pass you by. Be still and allow the positive energy all around you to lead you in the right direction.

POSITIVE THOUGHTS, POSITIVE VIBES.

TODAY IS YOUR DAY

It is often said, "Tomorrow is not promised and today is short." It is easier said than done to focus on today and not think about tomorrow.

We spend most of our time planning for the future and not enjoying the blessings we have today. In the blink of an eye, your world can turn upside down.

Today is the day. Love more, live more and pray more. Hold no regrets because what God has in store for tomorrow is not yours to control. He has given you today to see your blessings.

POSITIVE THOUGHTS, POSITIVE VIBES.

TAKE A MINUTE TO ENJOY WHAT GOD HAS GIVEN US!

KEEP SMILING, LET YOUR LIGHT SHINE!

Matthew 5:16

*In the same way, let your light shine
before others, that they may see
your good deeds and glorify
your Father in heaven.*

DO IT!

START A BUSINESS,

~ WRITE A BOOK ~

GOD GAVE YOU TODAY SO GO OUT AND LIVE IT!

WE ALL HAVE A GIFT TO SHARE!

Philippians 4:8

Finally, brothers and sisters,
whatever is true,
whatever is noble,
whatever is right,
whatever is pure,
whatever is lovely,
whatever is admirable
—if anything is excellent
or praiseworthy
—think about such things.

ABOUT THE AUTHOR

Preston Mitchum Jr. has dedicated his life to giving back and making a difference. Born in Bronx, New York his family moved to Langley Park, MD in 1981.

His family established the Mitchum Lawn and Landscaping business shortly after. This is where his father, Mitchum Sr. worked for over 30 years, created beautiful lawns and established relationships throughout the community.

Preston Jr. is a graduate of Towson State University where he took his love for video and became an 18 year veteran news photographer for WMAR-TV in Baltimore, Maryland.

During this time, he founded The PMJ Foundation to create change in the Baltimore community. The foundation's vision is to impact families through programs and services that offer positive growth. The foundation has served thousands throughout Maryland.

With the passing of his father, Preston has taken over the family business and will continue to provide the quality service that his family established for many years.

~

A portion of the proceeds of this book
will support the programs that the
PMJ Foundation offers.

~

This book is dedicated to Preston's
two wonderful sons, Carter and Harrison.

~

Preston hopes that the positive message this
book has to offer will impact thousands and
create positive vibes that we all can feel.

THE PMJ FOUNDATION

PRESENTING POSSIBILITIES
FOR BRIGHTER FUTURES

The PMJ Foundation's Career Awareness Project (CAP) after-school program brings the outside professional world into the classroom. Community volunteers present their careers to our participants which engage our at-risk youth to explore the infinite possibilities of college and career choices that are available.

~

To learn more about the PMJ Foundation please visit: **www.pmjfoundation.org**

ERIN GO BRAGH
Publishing

Erin Go Bragh Publishing publishes various genres of books for numerous authors. Their portfolio consists of a 1200 page Vietnamese to English Dictionary, Historical fiction, an award-winning children's educational series, multiple adult novels and memoires, tween adventure stories, as well as Christian Fiction. Their objective is to promote literacy and education through reading and writing.

www.ErinGoBraghPublishing.com
Canyon Lake, Texas

REFERENCES

Brooks Hatlen *movie* "Shawshank Redemption", *1994*

Michael Jackson *song "Man in the Mirror" written by Siedah Garrett and Glen Ballard, from the album* Bad, *1987*

TLC *song* "Waterfalls" *Album* "CrazySexyCool*"1994*

Kirk Franklin *i song* "Melodies from Heaven" *Album* "Songs from the Storm, Volume 1 *"2006*

Reference: Ben E King *song "Stand By Me" from the single released in 1961*

Reference: *Song by* Anthony Brown *and Group Therapy*

Made in USA - Kendallville, IN
23695_9781941345610
12.08.2021 1539